Eleni Cay is a Slovakian-born poet living in Manchester, UK. Her poems were published in two pamphlets – *Colours of the Swan* and *Autumn Dedications* – and featured in MK Calling 2013 & 2015. She's widely published in anthologies such as *Mother's Milk*, poetry magazines such as *Envoi* and *Atticus Review*, and on the 'best poetry videos on the web' ('Moving Poems'). Eleni is currently studying the MA in Creative Writing at Manchester Metropolitan University.

About John Minahane

John Minahane was born near Baltimore in the south of Ireland in 1950. From the age of 18, when a short story of his was published, he occasionally produced poetry and short stories, but mainly he was fascinated by history and the literature of the old Irish language. His principal work on this subject is *The Christian Druids: on the filid or philosopher-poets of Ireland* (1993, republished 2008), which includes some of the finest ancient poems with English translations.

In 1996 Minahane moved to Slovakia. His first major undertaking as a translator from Slovak was a selection of the poems and literary essays of Ladislav Novomeský (*Slovak Spring*, 2004). Later published works include selections from the lyrics of Milan Rúfus, *To Bear the Burden and Sing* (2008); *Six Slovak Poets* (2010); Ján Buzássy's *Eighteen Poems* (2012); and the classic novel *Three Chestnut Horses* by Margita Figuli (2014). Recent poetry collections which he has translated include Jozef Leikert's *The Cobweb of Being* (2015), Štefan Kuzma's *whisper* (2016), and the anti-war poems written at the outbreak of World War 1 by Pavol Országh Hviezdoslav, *Bloody Sonnets* (2016).

A BUTTERFLY'S TREMBLING IN THE DIGITAL AGE

Eleni Cay

Translated by John Minahane

PARTHIAN

Parthian, Cardigan SA43 1ED
www.parthianbooks.com
First published in 2017
Originally published in Slovak by ČAKANKA, in Nitra, Slovakia, in 2013.
© Eleni Cay 2017
This book has received a subsidy from SLOLIA Committee,
the Centre for Information on Literature in Bratislava, Slovakia.
ISBN 978-1-910901-94-6
Cover image by Mgr. art. Samuel Juriš
Cover design by Robert Harries
Typeset by Elaine Sharples
Printed in EU by Pulsio SARL
Published with the financial support of the Welsh Books Council
British Library Cataloguing in Publication Data
A cataloguing record for this book is available from the British Library.

Dedicated to all who are seeking, losing and finding love and beauty in the digital age.

Contents

1 Revolution
2 Welcome, digital!
3 Black-and-white QR Codes
4 Universal Dictionaries
5 Scentless Words
6 Digital Thoughts
8 Face-book
9 New Forms, Old Coins
10 iClouds Lives
12 Women for Ads
13 Dead Souls
14 Playfully…
15 Curves, Curves, Curves
16 Love Online
17 Universal Love
19 Boxes for Feelings
20 A Sad Story in a Digital Bin
21 Postcard Without a Stamp
22 Caribbean Blue
23 Welcome to Your All-inclusive Resort!
24 Loving Texts
25 Springbreeze.sk
26 Cretan Queen
27 The Natural's Being Lost…
28 Thoughts Without Wrapping
29 Photographers
31 The Hunt for Authenticity
32 Through the Black Fields
33 Temples of Inviolate Thoughts
34 Love That's In the Cocoon

35	Spring Freeze
36	Tears on a Damp Stone
37	A Bloody Prayer
39	Marsh
40	Asking for Alms
42	The Angel and Devil In Us
43	While on the Angel's Wings
44	Slave of Your Own Choice
45	Clown on a unicycle
46	Tempus tantum temporarium est
47	The Boy's Already on the Move
48	Memories
49	Jozef Mak
50	Footprints in the Snow
51	Les témoignages
52	Undertow
53	Carpe diem
54	Andante
55	Door to the Keyhole
56	Home Is the Hands…
57	And Joyfully God Sowed The Golden Grain…
58	Codex of Life
60	The Essence of Life Is Movement
61	For the Girl Who's Forever in Love, Madame la Nature
62	Circles

Revolution

Some don't understand, and some have come to terms.
Others bow down before the screen.
The change came silently.

As in war
quick-marching here and now,
crudely
and with no blueprints telling how,
we're learning Facebook, emails, and so on.
Like the tin soldier cast without a leg,
on the virtual field we've all been left half-done.

New hybrid of the image and the word.
Like every revolution
the digital has come:
with the young, and spurred.

Welcome, digital!

A few years ago thoughts spoke
with pen and paper.
Now a small box can be their medium.
No need for tickets, dressing, scheduling:
from stage to auditorium,
when and wherever endlessly,
thoughts wing.

The digital holds everything, all sorts.
Chance meetings, lies, creeds, travellers' reports.

Maybe it's fine
that your message bleeps in the quiet of a wood.
One curses and the other thinks it good.
One photographs, the other writes some pages.
For their feelings people
always seek refuges.

So welcome, digital!
My fantasy's new well and source.
As if it went on water,
level, smooth,
an aircraft runs its course.
I welcome it and then,
dazzled by the hopes,
lose myself therein.

Black-and-white QR Codes

A gesture tells the woman
she has to twirl, in a waltz or reel.
And an icon may suffice for what you feel.

Weary of writing,
you gaze out on the square,
your sentence still resounding,
your fists clenching on air.
Man, do you stuff yourself because
your expiry date is near?
And quickly scribble an extra clause
to a deal that leads to catastrophe?

Billboard words are tumbling,
and all that time will yet unwrap
for lives' episodes.
The path to the church is crumbling.
We're praying in new codes.

A noisy drier substitutes
for colourful washing out the back.
Currently what we produce
is sort of white-and-black.

The poem's lost in the dictate of new modes,
with no colour, no life –
like those QR codes.

Universal Dictionaries

Like an old word processor you underline
the letters we call *iks* and *ypsilon*;
pencil in hand, you want to go back to words
that lend the poem rhyme and tone.

The more you learn,
the harder 'tis to deafen your sharp ear;
you understand
and won't let slip the random words you hear.

So, winners are the ones
who quickly grasp the new vocabulary…
… old words have said their fill,
but their wisdom hasn't grown to a giant tree.

You can escape from anything, my dear,
from anything… but change.
With earphones on,
you pretend you don't see, don't hear,
that you're relaxing, alone,
though your gossipy schoolfriend lies
on the beachtowel next your own.

Word stocks are sparser for the original.
Foreign tongues all sound more identical.

Scentless Words

"I love you so much I've put you on my desktop!"
Weird, these novel declarations.
To the poem, somehow, they don't mean a thing.

Forced rhymes and conversations.
And always ending, "right, okay, you'll ring?"

No need to say with whom, where or where to.
Males, females, everywhere
GPS follows you.

My phone shines in the dark of drunken discotheques.
It's a new age, no tenderness in sex.

iWatch on eyes, ears clappered,
you flee your world pell-mell.
Your sweat cuts through
the stink of puke on the carousel.

Digital Thoughts

Thoughts that used to inspire poems
were there on Twitter,
as if choked on collars.
Sometimes targeted and clear,
sometimes like half-chewed morsels
of a child's dinner.

Granny, you know, today the important news
is what's not spoken of.
Because everyone informs, writes, publishes;
his unlimited-tariff mobile's never off.

So what'll you offer the poem in digital?
Frilly couplets in black-and-white numerals?
An auction for most likes?

The trembling butterfly won't even dare fly in.
An international airport makes you feel so small,
an ordinary nobody-nothing.

You feel you can't please kids with tricks of an old-time clown.
Those basketfuls of oranges would surely weigh you down.

Flight routes of mighty aeroplanes tangle like balls of thread.
No special things to share, no meals of rationed food.

Do you blaze, do you amaze, poet? – with what?
Without a stage, without a plug,
the conjuror would stand
on the corner, just like that.

He put fragments of joy into a mind's great hurt.
Gave little moments an eternal worth.

So too, the digital
tunes imagination's harp,
raises the value of surprise,
pares the pencils of expectancy till sharp.

Face-book

To him above and all beneath
you lend the face that's yours.
And it surprises you
that the digital screen
is scribbled with prayers.

Fascinated for eons
with faces that are ours.
That's why you're so drawn now to monitors.

Face-book – book of faces,
new smile-frames for mortals!
Pleased with the proffered gallery-space,
ever-new faces hang upon the portal.

How many times have you changed your profile shot?
Here I'm at work, here's me with cooking pots…
Ephemeral fashion makes me smile.
I'm waiting till time changes,
by a gradual greening,
the town statues' clothing style.

Through cultures, societies,
time makes no divide.
Time sees everywhere,
in slogans you can't hide.
So don't be cheap, reveal yourself by stages,
don't make pebbles of your marble with mad hacks,
and don't betray in a self-portrait
what your memory lacks.

New Forms, Old Coins

So it's arrived, the revolution of forms.
And you urgently invent new metaphors.
In order that the digital-crust boxes
can rest awhile from their labours.

Mr. Invention,
from the digital craze will you quench the weak's thirst?
Will you prove you're a sharer even in the worst?

A little beggar
spotted a wealthy tourist;
weak as a stamp without a letter,
he followed him, hopping on one leg:
"Money, sir, money" –
give some of the coins in your pocket, I beg!

"What's your name, sir, where from?" a beggar girl cries.
"In your own language I'll sing you a song of love!"
Ah, but will that suffice for a coin from "sir"?
The old crown in his pocket jingles, ready to move.

Enquiring glances of love and fortune;
uncertain, weak, they remained,
those who had hitherto enquired without a question.

iClouds Lives

You used to play chess.
There was a sequence, boundaries were clean.
Now without working you may have success –
just tap upon a screen.

On that black field you caress
with the same touch
your bank, your family, your girl,
in no particular hierarchy.
Will you skip the football match
while your son sings to you at the school festival?
Are you the loser,
or our child,
or granddad lying in hospital?
Do we rob each other of fondles and smiles?

Another coin in the bottomless bag, flip, flip.
Can it bite off the colours on the broad brush tip?

Like a pony pulling a lightly-loaded cart,
with suitcase you hurry
through airports,
chasing virtual miles,
exchanges, swaps, imaginary property.

I take it I may have your online albums without cost.
I won't guess name or age of a digital face:
for what's still forming, numbers won't be true.
Glowing and molten, like the moon aloft –
human, that's you.

Suddenly you took fright at your own face
on the macbook's black screen.
The bitten apple greeting you each morning
reminds you that you're incomplete.
You break a piece from the unrotted part;
you sail upon white dust of human bones
like clouds in the sky,
desperate, perplexed.
The life of perfect happiness on earth
was not composed according to the sketch.

Women for Ads

Ah, beauties of the moment, models!
Everywhere it's you that someone watches.
Mirrors,
admirers' eyes,
digital lenses.

From outside you're so weather-washed,
your wrappings have turned quite transparent.
My starlets, modelled actresses,
mere empty oysters
brought in by a sea current.

And *you*, designer now and tailor,
stand awhile and think.
And do not shorten their ways home.
Let us not call truth
what are only platforms,
things of foam.

Dead Souls

Like the humming-bird that wished to drink
the lake's water,
the old poet remained thunder-struck
in his aviary of paper.

D'you worry if digital's good for metaphor?

In northern seas the fish are less diverse,
in southern they've more colour.
Forget the hierarchies.
In the digital everyone publishes,
they borrow the cookie cutter.

Time, that miser wind,
scatters the children's sandpit at one go.
Above the high hills you saw
you'd been flying too low.

With fins in the sky,
with wings in the sea,
God's messengers gather
thoughts through the country.
They're still warm, you can tell they died in disquiet.
They did not know – Lord, forgive them all –
that both form and content make souls immortal.

Playfully…

We press buttons
on smartphones and tablets,
like our little ones.
Children and buttons, those gates to marvels,
always have been close;
you too are playing now
and you seem equally engrossed.

Click-click, let there be song,
let there be light,
reminding you of you.

A girl was playing sudoku,
click-clickety-click;
off without her the express train flew.

Click-clickety-click.
A while ago a boy leaped in the rain,
startling the little dog that was trying his tricks.

Today he sits at home by a neon screen,
ipad in hand,
a nappy on his behind.

Curves, Curves, Curves

Curves, curves, curves.
The kids are drawing clouds.
Once they reminded you of hearts.
Now "wifis!" you'll exclaim aloud.

Curves, curves, curves.
The first cars were boxes with sharp angles.
Today we've rounded them and even smoothed the handles.

The thirteenth chamber's ever easier to enter.
And returns to childhood ever bitterer and harder.

Yes, I know – time will round those oblong texts.
But somehow it's amorphous, that period "between" or "toward".
Hearts cut from love, they want to fit them into squares.
Impossible, absurd.

Love Online

Back then you had to put on weight and grow a beard.
Now, to get your false passport, the tricks are much improved;
and since they digitalised its voice,
it's easier to be deceived in love.

Honey, I miss you here! –
(with coloured smiley at the tail).
The little modern postman
brings the news through hill and dale.

Thus the internet made the far near and out-of-sight partners seen.
Thus lovers became used to kissing through the screen.

I've noticed wrinkles on romantics' brows.
They know: not many jazzmen can play… Chopin, say.
Love's perfumes are disordered.
You won't digitalise, virtualise love-making in the hay.

Universal Love

That new world of love –
like a garden table,
plastic and artificial.
He wanted to tickle her nose with ice-cream,
but wasn't able
to find the keyboard symbol.

Since we've been dining
at the virtual board
you sound like an old troubadour under the balcony, dear.
With a voice hoarse from singing
you gild new cages for inexperienced birds.
And you shake the virtual sack;
a herald of democracy,
you want to emulate all those who've got rich quick.

And everything tires you. Even going into detail with me.
So you've squashed me to universality.

Love, advise me,
how to speak,
how to serve,
how to let my darling have you back.

Should I ring?
Or better send a text?
Or will I email him that feeling?
So we have back-up
and more time to receive?
No, he prefers skype…

We paralyse with new communication
what once came from our mouths easily, "just like that".

Help me, Love, I've no idea what wrap
I'm to dress myself in;
let him dump that world-wide-web!
Love, send him back to me again,
I beg you with the one-word universal *Help*…

Boxes for Feelings

You send thoughts
to barrack squares.
In SMS
they twist about
like startled bears.

He isn't writing – no time, battery, signal?
At the silent reply
you solved a different riddle.

Unified in emoticons
you send your moods, your vacillating glances
and childish fears.

We carry boxes in our pockets for smiles, for tears.

You conquer me at distance,
rejuvenate with a wind-blown kiss.

The wrapped feeling
came all those miles
in the digital beak
of an SMS.

A Sad Story in a Digital Bin

We drenched our love with quarrels.
In text messages and emails
and new digital imprints,
I find us too and our event.

Not a bit left –
the weeping's dried
and the footprints in the soul,
mud-smeared.

Everything's lost
in a digital bin.
The lovers' letters
and the hidden tear.

Postcard Without a Stamp

The SMS rolls over hills and through seas,
enclosing puffed-up expectations.
From hand to hand, as in olden days,
it brings joy and disillusion,
and fits experiences' colours
into a phrase.

Darling, how I miss you here!
I send you long-distance love
with just one finger,
no strain, no cramp.

A digital postcard
without the exotic stamp.

Caribbean Blue

The incredible blue
of the Caribbean sea.
You cannot explain it to the eyes.

"So capture me!"
and I prepare the shot.
"Quick, or I'll be on someone's Facebook page."

What do we still have that's original,
unpublished, in ourselves?
Azure sea,
I dreamed a dream of you.

I know I'll never capture in poems
what I saw with closed eyes.

Welcome to Your All-inclusive Resort!

They parked their armoured coaches in front of the hotels.
On an uninhabited island they moored new residents' yachts.
Glutted, they continue heaping up their plates;
they take in bucketfuls and keep loosening their belts.

New age kings,
whose thirst abolishes opening hours:
golden neck-chains hanging,
engraved bracelets on their wrists,
in their all-inclusive resorts
they're miserable as men in jail.
Rich = convicts… no great difference exists.

Behind barbed wire, the people of the South
have mounted swings for the moneyed ones.
But the penguins aren't able to swing high.
Boring tales of the dollar, in monotone.
Like blood from a mosquito's mouth
meanness dribbles from their lips.
The greed in their bellies flies near Earth, too near.
The villager can't understand;
he rocks with mirth, he grins from ear to ear.

Loving Texts

No need of a telescope
for beauties far away.
Wireless, we declare our love;
across the ocean comes his amorous gaze.

"Are you asleep? No? Write to me!"
Strew me with long-distance kisses.
All that once might have been memories and wishes.

Morning, evening we're calling, no cessation,
so we can say
what once took years to grow
into a declaration.

The lad was bashful
when he invited her for icecream first.
How glad he is the iphone hides his blush!

Somehow email, SMS,
make talk an easier task,
as if the natural human
got lost in a social mask.

So you don't recognise such love? — you know no other sort?
And who will tell you? — She? A pal? Or time?
Ah, Time! Even Time's a small boy in a big game.
And rarely does he knock politely upon doors.
He enters lovers' homes without warning or reserve;
suddenly, unforeseen, access is easy there.
We have not guarded them against ourselves.

Springbreeze.sk

At the hilltop, sweaty, what delights you most is the signal.
An SMS! — even here, my darling's got the range!

And nowadays we get acquainted on the web,
admire or mock each other on a page.

There are people
who fit life into a single webpage.
And call those worlds
"Me.com".

Which doesn't work for some:
"I'm too dimensional for this!"
They won't be stowed in a suitcase.
They roam the world, name-tagged with no name.

Modern medicine doesn't heal, just patches.
— She hasn't yet given birth,
but she's planned her son's first online photo-batches.

Quicker than you thought,
you shrink your world to new coordinates.
Longing memories of home can't be sustained:
you save your thoughts to new addresses.

The precious moment complained
to a fragrant breeze:
They've put me on a webpage,
squashed down, squeezed.

Cretan Queen

So fertile once,
the green garden's overgrown with weeds.
They felled the trees,
and it's hard to find replacement, hard indeed.

They say, let's weave our rods, togetherness will give strength.
In the hubbub you can't hear a pure note, see a colour, or feel anything.

Assertion, progress, binds the yellow-skinned,
poverty binds poverty.
My Europe, what binds you?

Houses precarious as Lego sets
are bonded along mouldering streets.

Too old for change, too beautiful to disappear.
Young people knock on a door;
through the keyhole
an unquiet poet peers.

The Natural's Being Lost…

Earphones in place
and tapping out modern Morse,
the boy didn't hear the delicate scream
as he trod on the arm of the grass.

Earth's only hopping on a magpie-leg.
Too many flowers, weeds,
international currencies.
Too people-heavy, on the animal count too light.
Do you do this deliberately, God, with your great oversight?

Higher than the marble statue in the square,
we have portrayed Nature on a pedestal of beauty past compare.

And like the pigeon that may sit at times on her shoulder,
man too dies of grains that are wrapped in poison.
Man has become a tourist
in his own garden.

Thoughts Without Wrapping

You don't just sense — you're well aware,
the gaudy packaging disgusts you.
But though its wrapper makes no sense,
the snack is tasty and it boosts you.
And so you buy, buy, without stop
and fill the kitchen space at home,
until you stink like dustmen's trucks
from all the junk that you consume.

Is this the way to knowledge
of others or yourself?
Like an armature on the back of hope,
you carry thoughts on pilgrimage;
you lighten days with travels of novel scope.

The space of what's material narrows;
you make no secret now of your desire.
You're on a date with the credit card on your table.
Below ground and above, travel's for hire.

For your first flight into space, what're you packing?
Ah, my dear human — just yourself, without a wrapping.

Photographers

You invent ever more perfect lenses to capture instants.
And you have less resources
for the moments
that you should have lived.

Lenses from all sides —
you know celebrity delirium.
The paparazzo paralyses moments,
kills them right before your eyes.
And he snaps everything — facts, feelings, dreams.
Young cameraman without a genuine theme.

Once people had experience within them, as in tunnels.
Now all is digitalised, even royal scrolls.

Without these snaps
what'll be left of people?
Kings run naked
in the digital vestibule.

How quickly must a reporter
run to catch himself at an unexpected moment?
He's flower and bee, he gets drunk on his own nectar,
zooms, crinkles his nose,
wants to get near the gaze
hidden in the half-shut eye.

Thus the photographer forces moments
and makes the lens, already little, smaller.
He's like a question mark
with that heavy gear on his shoulder.

Strip an exhausted moment naked?
The paparazzo can.

By the angle of vision you know the wisdom of the man.

The Hunt for Authenticity

There's a madness like in love:
"Unique, you'll find it nowhere else, it's just for you".
The authenticity hunt has sealed up many eyes.

Young and old wait as if to be resurrected,
they've changed their values like their coats.
Is that OK and where's the boundary?
You can't see it; you're disconcerted
by the new-old merchants.

Swap and change is the slogan of the day;
we're simply making deals, now as before,
to gain, gain, gain;
without blinking an eye
we rebottle, relabel, the old wine.

Like a blind man afraid of obstacles,
you narrow the choices down;
you go back in time to experience something new,
you seek in the country what you buried in town.

Don't promise anything authentic, poem.
Slogans will sound, but don't succumb.
Hold onto what you've saved for years.

God knows that journeying to the authentic
is a cross too heavy for man to bear.

Through the Black Fields

Afternoon love's pale pink breaks through:
having roamed the whole world, weary,
it seeks a small corner desperately,
for its painful plight.
With black ink on white paper, I write
lines of fidelity to you.

Just for a moment ignite my flame,
give me your shoulder to recline on,
burn in a microsecond the long-borne crosses,
let me forget those efforts at better
and more efficient and faster…

Generation of black coffees and touch screens,
I'm afraid of your, of our, "tomorrow".

You'll say, "Ah, there was always something, and something will
 always be".
But memories have paled and hope's been buried.
A young girl no longer believes in the absolute;
the heart in her young breast's dismembered.

"Multi"-freedom as a swap for love.
And without questions asked they raped that little woman Hope.

God, I beg you, kill us without agony.

Temples of Inviolate Thoughts

I am tired.
Sated with texts, sounds, words.
Like a drug I reach for the internet.
To tangle myself awhile in my web.

Permit me to switch off,
go online and be lost.
In the stifling city
I'd like to let still-living memory rest.
Once I used to hide it in empty churches.
In silence – no bells, no monitors.
With eyes refreshed,
the soul could afterwards sustain
the stress of further slogans.
Vainly today I seek a haven for experiences deceased.
Pressure from all sides – play, spin, write…

You float on round coracles in transparent waters
towards the king's palace and the thoughts hidden there.
The temple of the original
may be entered only in a pair.

Inspiration innocently surges
to you from me;
I have found peace, I have found myself,
as on the surface of a sea.

Love That's In the Cocoon

Time was when you kept a diary:
like a butterfly catcher you captured thoughts.
Now when they fly,
in black-and-white
they're digitalised as soon as caught.

You lie in layers through the pages;
never does it cross your mind
how day by day
you strangle time.

"Digital natives" Prensky called that generation.
They shrink the mosaic of days to SMS-diminution.

The internet spreads its sticky web
in seconds, no more;
you seek your reality in treacherous allure.
Friends in your pocket; work and family
personalised and always on;
more and more you make the box *sine qua non*.

Depends on you how many thoughts,
how many smiles and tears are lost –
it's up to you, not fate.

Whether love that is in the cocoon
gets entangled or flies
forth from the wide net.

Spring Freeze

I find it so sad.
That even Marley doesn't cheer you any more.
That all you'll say of Spring's first flowers is:
"Ah, fragile beauty. Quickly come, and quickly go."
And even when we make love,
you're like a puppet to be played.
Unresponsive,
passionless,
glassy-eyed.
In Spring you find yourself in autumn, dear.

Days as scripted arrive and depart,
you put them in the wardrobe like ironed sheets.
For you nothing, nothing's absolute.

Your empty gaze upon my window troubles me;
it's reflected upon pavements with no verge.
Pale blue agony that has no hope –
with you, I am pained by that knowledge.

God crushed into a million little motes
trembles desperately in Chopin's note.
You have remained unfaithful to no one and to all.

Tears on a Damp Stone

Outside the window stand the trees,
uncomprehending, taciturn.
They are resigned.

That one unfinished dawn
has ceased bleeding, but still hurts.

An arm is sagging,
the hand no longer holds or cuts the stone.
Indifferently we shift from foot to foot,
we believe in nothing and no one,
there's a void, starved of the air.

The ages fixed their values in positions now lost,
all that's left of the steps is stones without verges.

Nothing matters,
so brief is our day.
Perfunctorily you seek balance,
but every stone is slippery.

Faster and faster the spiral turns,
man, ever-less-human, mounting to the stars.

Today there are no steps, just trajectory.

A Bloody Prayer

Night was wiping
translucent tears
from the cold face
of the grass.

That lad was not afraid.
He boarded the bus like any other morning.
Just that his hands sweated a little more –
they left the handrail damp.
What was he thinking?
Thoughts of his paradise, or the void, no one and nothing?
He blew himself up in the crowd,
among children, lovers, who were happy then.
Just like that.
Because they'd told him.
Because they'd given him an empty promise,
they'd found that tender point in the human soul.
…
You no longer notice, where and how many dead.
A blown-off shoe
wet in a pool of blood.
Tears slide down furrows on a child's face at a funeral.

Lord, reclaim us, admit us back to you.
I beg you on my knees,
return to your great work, to man.
Or stifle love,
drown it forever in mother's milk.
…
God does not listen.
The white narcissus has lost itself in the water.

With a face that's no one's,
man enters heaven.

Marsh

Ruin's sitting
at love's table.
These days, an expected guest.

Because we've sacrificed soul to form,
and bells are always pealing
for some child being laid to rest.

To choose silence,
withdraw into the shell?
Or to seek, and bleed, on that unequal battleground?
Who'll offer me advice,
when the hungry do not know, the full don't want?
And both of these are always to be found.

We pay for knowledge
with the coin of freedom. Certainly,
if we had none, time's stream would surge
to the future more pacifically.

You drowned yourself, human, in the river.
The tears on the old snuffbox turned all rusty.

I ask you, God, disclose
to us your pure eternal waters,
somewhere to draw from, somewhere to cease to worry.

Not tomorrow but today, this harsh
moment when everywhere's just marsh,
marsh,
marsh.

Asking for Alms

Maybe each of us will grow up one day
and admit
that the greatest obstacle
isn't the others, or evil fate.
We ourselves are the block.

For years your hair's been falling out,
it softens to snow
and you feel
you no longer have frames for so many works.

There used to be many. Plenty. Of everything.
And what he took from us – let be!
On our journey we were stubborn, perverse.
We lamented that we didn't have,
we desired or dreamed of, something else.

With the sweet honey of hopes
we glued our future,
plunged into unknown rivers
with open embrace.
Slowly you sober at the rivermouth
and see how you and your desires were striving against the
    grain.
You and your human choice.

What reality took from dreams was yours
when you drank the wine of love.
Now crumpled, with fluff on your head,
for your memories you want to build
bridges over the wrinkles' dry grooves.

With loss of desires you paid the price for life.
Now you only ask alms. With begging words
and bald-headed bowl
you wait for death, for your reward.

The Angel and Devil In Us

At night after the tour there must be fire.
It veils in mystery
what binds people primally:
heat, a story, touch.

Tamed fire in the candle attended lovers' nights.
By day it proudly dreamed of Olympic heights.

You sit by the hearth and feed the colours,
you glimpse hidden stories leaping up and down.
Montgolfier looked in there and thought of a balloon.

You turn red, you turn blue,
daily with tears you quench small blazes.
Ah, marvellous human faces!
Angel in us and devil too,
perfection *par excellence*.

Both belong to you, man,
they warm you, they gnaw you by night.
Fire and water:
thanks only to them you are man,
not a chrysalis in a cocoon.

While on the Angel's Wings

After long wandering
the soul returns to Earth.
People then are glad
of their Love's ripe worth.

On joining reality,
the baby screams out loud.
He's telling you, for your lock he is the key.

He's saying dance,
while your portion of bread's dwindling;
eat your fill,
before the little mite in you starts shrilling.

Live. Full tilt. Till the cry changes to silence.
And breathe to the last word left in you.

While your soul on the wings of the angel
pianissimo returns whence it flew.

Slave of Your Own Choice

From countless stars the wise astronomer picks one.
And on a single horse he wagers all his hope.
No mother ever lays six children in one lap.
A thousand options, you must choose: a few, or none.

Fuddled human animal.
Perceives, and feels, and would like all,
and cannot choose.

Love at least seals,
fences the amorous space.

The rest is yours in solitude.

In an unending lottery,
to adjust for Lady Luck
a frame carved out with sweat and blood.

Clown on a unicycle

On a tin bicycle
with big front wheel
made by the wizard of Oz,
you ride on the grooved rim
of the rough coin of days.

Sometimes – it's his prerogative –
chance drops in to visit,
and down a sunbeam slope
he leads you to a land
of naive hope.
He promises love, he's brought
sweet rainbows for your thought.

But the wind of ordinariness soon takes over
and cools like a slap on the face, or squall of sleet.
Or like that time when we'd made love,
and you opened the window onto the noisy street.

Tempus tantum temporarium est

If all of life
is only a field ploughed long ago
with eternal furrows and
wounded in the storms,
by now I'm not surprised.
Gradually I forget everything,
but here and there a small faith forms,
sprouting in green memories.
You've forgotten the seeds of hope you sowed
way back – irony once again!

And if you call the wind Time
and Lord of him who sows the grain,
you'll change your prayers soon.

Let there be fewer springtimes from now on,
just an Indian sun in the ferns, at afternoon.

The Boy's Already on the Move

With a linden sun
like liquid honey,
you glue memories
of boyhood summer.

Barefoot in stubble-fields, away
from worries, out with friends and free…
Ah, there's no such field today.
The barley's hair is rippling in the evening,
you count the little grains, those nameless feelings.

And then, when your river dries,
you look into your memories.
Through grey hair tightly tied
you let a young butterfly loose,
thankful to have so many halts
before reaching silence, your terminus.

On a long-ago-painted table
the old gramophone hums,
slowly,
then ever louder
at a world that screams.
Do you remember how we danced?
Magdalena was still innocent, she blushed.
Those prickly soul-fibres,
you fondle them from on high,
while galloping down a side-street,
everyday life goes by.

Memories

> *"Alone, a person breaks off memories like pieces of bread."*
> Milan Rúfus, *Letter to a Woman*

Graven with diamond into time's soft face,
experience lasts in memory,
listening to a far-off voice.

Fragile-winged, at times it brings what's rarest for you,
a flight over the land of knowledge that you've passed through.

So too now
at my piano, while I play yesterday's notes,
beside me there's an empty chair.
I set my remembrances there,
what memory brings,
note after note;
at the jubilee concert
played memories fade out.

Till ears ache from so much declaration.
Words conceal, and more is told by silence.
I play on,
as I realise I'll never be alone.
We are never alone in that beautiful loneliness with these:
I am wealthy, I am immortal with memories.

Jozef Mak*

There is a land
where people breakfast on knowledge,
lunch on feelings,
and break off bits of memory for supper.

Some who live in that land look at a springtime bud
and guess how much it may weigh.
Others ponder how to turn it into money.
Others again stand still, not knowing how to give thanks for all
    that beauty.

And all will arrive at the goal,
with bellies empty or full.
So, man, what makes you man?
What counts on the other shore?

On a church tower a bell has groaned:
you acknowledge you're no more
than a single unripe ear, a grain
to be sown in the earth again.

With desires high as the stars' track,
the ordinary Jozef Mak.

Jozef Mak, lit. 'Joseph Poppyseed', the 'man-of-the-million', a novel by the Slovak writer Jozef Cíger Hronský.

Footprints in the Snow

Artists burn their lightbulbs late at night.
Hunched over supple words,
they try to lend them feelings' weight:

in the miniature gauze of art
a song that has come through its pain,
captured images, still lives,
those "things" that teach you to fly high and higher again.

They strike banality's rust off hopeful gold.
With brushstrokes they slow down too-hurrying time.
Thank you, thank you, artists young and old.

But will it be enough?
For all our faults, we sinners?
When they send troops to the front lines of the ordinary,
poem, can you bear not to be perversely tender?

Man, be an artist; create, invent.
And stay pure.
Pure as fresh snow.
Stride upon that. And there leave your prints.
Soon it will melt, as it must,
but you were first there, in that one moment first.

Do not give up in treacherous snow.
Hope onwards, push your laden cart along.
That snow sings differently to everyone.
For you it'll choose its most delightful song.

Les témoignages

Like two lovers in a crowd whom a magnolia scent unites,
inconspicuous yet precise,
Madame la Muse comes down from heaven.

On wings of dandelion she carries
the souls of Chopin, Rúfus.
That one prelude proves,
that one strophe testifies: he is.
The grass-stalks with their swan-necks bow,
admitting silently that only she knows how:
to renew mankind, to give time back to love.

In quiet hills of untouched beauty
the poet sought the Muse,
but found shards only. Shards of love from us, in us.

Undertow

Like the sigh of wood
that, blue and narrow,
parts from the water
in its veins
and succumbs to fire,
rhythmically
with narrow pen
a man inscribes
new life in a woman,
mother-to-be.

On white canvas
time sews experience,
variations on attested themes.

How many of these waves can one woman take in?
By the law that Nature and we have written,
a girl seeks her being
and by the shore weeps tears of healing.

How beautiful to weep by the sea:
it drinks up everything,
all pains, loves, losses,
all these human constructs equally.

The girl wants to understand love,
but too much girlish hope survives.
The wave divides:
it carries away all
her tears, and brings back salt, salt for her eyes,
while rhythmic, into her, her darling falls
and falls.

Carpe diem

White ribbons floated across the sky,
they fell in songburst from the mouths of birds.
Slow night turns pink at sunset, and day ends.

But until the nightingale's concert starts,
there's a boundary moment.
Like a first kiss on girlish cheeks,
full of hope, innocent.

Are you losing her, now that her name is named?
Or have you made her lovely with that word?

Sublime in motion,
clothed in lilies,
Desire surges in its parts.
Do not grasp it, do not name it:
you'll be snarled in the spider's nets.

You won't reach it by request or by hurried prayer.
Wait humbly – that's the language of fulfilled desire.
Andante, gentle and rounded.
In your concert, softly sounding.

And warming, as winter under the lamp
whose gentle glow
fell through parted lips
with flakes of snow.

Andante

A clear sky smooth as ice.
Oh to call Yagudin to her, let him come, pirouetting, to kiss.

The morning symphony starts slowly,
the red curtain rises.
What will the day bring?
Joys, disappointments?
Rising from his seat is the conductor, the sun.
What will life bring?
Sorrows, misfortune.

There's a slow drip of tears
as the strings kiss the thicket.
You feel like the boy who could see
that the emperor was naked.

A curious blackbird rustles in the bushes.
A moment ago these leaves were weeping dew,
but they smile for blackbird time.
And no one, no one discovers the change.
Just a soft pale red that tinges a rough-cut rhyme.

Door to the Keyhole

White sheets were drying in the yard
and the air had a scent of green hills.
I longed to go home.

To huddle in arms,
bury my nose in fragrant skin,
to count together,
how many, oh my God, how many have passed…

I go and I fling off time,
veils woven with tears.

How many losses
and how many wishes fulfilled?

In your eyes I see mine,
reflections of knowledge we share.
On my palmlines
quietly I return to dreams
that I blew out with last year's birthday candles.

I lie on an old bed
and long for the dreams of youth.
Tomorrow I need do nothing –
just rise and escape to school.
Naive ones, hopeful, free of care.

It's hard to rise from a warm bed,
with teddybear pressed to a child's face.
Can it be that I've cried again?
Strange that I'm in a grown-up body, strange.

Home Is the Hands…

Days fall,
one after the other,
like drops of warm rain.
A cheeky wind browses the book
that you're forgetting gradually.
Everything.
Everything that was good and dear to you.

The wave disturbs and again smoothes
the sand on the beach.
This moment and the next,
you think about your life.

And it appals you, how little you remember…
The glass marbles you've found
bear witness as in court.
Lord God, how much has been,
and again will be, forgotten?

Don't fret.
These few moments are as precious as pearls.
The ocean Time won't reach them,
they've fled far in ashore.
Aromatic as tobacco root,
unique as our mothers' hands,
they transport you to the stars.

And Joyfully God Sowed The Golden Grain…

Maybe you just don't think
that God could not have managed
to put part of himself in earthly things.
To conjure moments of Heaven
in all time's portionings.

In a sky of storms,
on summer's plains,
on wavecrests that the ocean forms.

In lovers' eyes that try to capture
distance, till their gazing pains.

Uncounterfeited golden rapture.

Codex of Life

Lifelong we scramble
towards the clouds,
pursuing the crown
on the trees' heads.

As the body firms,
so does the will,
ever higher to grow.
At the conclusion
our Mother Earth
draws us back home.

Autumn, gathering time, has come – you're scarcely even aware.
One by one friends vanish from your field,
and new, young, thrusting grains appear.

There's snow on Earth yearly, on average.
Delicate featherlets, curled into tufts, cover the stage.

And though truth dwells surprisingly near,
we're doing a long-distance run.
Blazing our trail in the white fluff,
we go round what's trodden.
Till at the hill's summit,
tamed sufficiently and humbled,
we see many a path
that we bypassed unseeing, drunk on our own breath.

Bent old men quietly
wait like columns
in a strict law.

Yet they're only humans.
What can we do? Humbly now…

The Essence of Life Is Movement

In the big city,
confusion, noise, movement,
the lost aroma of bread
that's never warm.
You seek your own self,
at so many addresses mislaid.

All just because of movement…
One plays only when the roulette wheel spins.
And drops are rain
only when they fall.
So don't blink:
run, risk, right to the brink.

One slip and you'll fall in the sea.
Those same drops will drown you,
the splendid summer rain.
On the move.
From above.

For the Girl Who's Forever in Love, Madame la Nature

You're always on parade.
Often I'm in awe –
as if your wardrobe had no end.
Daily you display new dresses
and leave the connoisseurs of beauty breathless.

Summer necklaces around the fold and through
the uplands, flower shawls and rings of dew.

My God, and when you're raging,
how well you can be lovely then!
As if doused in silver,
and a flash of golden hair now and again.

Thank you, Nature, for all your coloured moods.
Thank you, for how we're worth it to you yet.
To dress in finery each day, parade.
Hopeful. Disinterested. Just like that.

Circles

When the land is drawn in sharp contours,
framed by a bird in a mint breeze,
then, my God, I believe in you without question.
Like the sheepfold's small well,
I let your water pour over me,
and get drunk on my own glass of poison.

Till they arrive again.
Those days of godless ordinariness
deepen the furrow in the wound.
Without overblown sensitivity
I'll pay some tax to them when they come round.

I shall return my loans;
let others have wherewithal to plant and fell new forests.
May you continue to send blue rain to green addresses.

Thus I sail with you, God, in one circle
and no longer seek a new song.
Life beneath us, above us,
entering us, the pure surface.
Nothing lures me now, nothing pains.
I have all. I have had.
I shall have again.

Lightning Source UK Ltd.
Milton Keynes UK
UKOW01f0352311017
311903UK00001B/32/P